TIGER WOODS
MAKES MASTERS
HISTORY

by Doug Williams

Greatest Events in
SPORTS HISTORY

www.abdopublishing.com

Published by Abdo Publishing, a division of ABDO, PO Box 398166, Minneapolis, Minnesota 55439. Copyright © 2015 by Abdo Consulting Group, Inc. International copyrights reserved in all countries. No part of this book may be reproduced in any form without written permission from the publisher. SportsZone™ is a trademark and logo of Abdo Publishing.

Printed in the United States of America, North Mankato, Minnesota
092014
012015

THIS BOOK CONTAINS
RECYCLED MATERIALS

Cover Photo: Dave Martin/AP Images
Interior Photos: Dave Martin/AP Images, 1, 18, 28, 30, 33, 36; David J. Phillip/AP Images, 4; Bettmann/Corbis, 6; AP Images, 9; Chris O'Meara/AP Images, 10; Bob Galbraith/AP Images, 13; Amy Sancetta/AP Images, 15, 27, 40; Charles Dharapak/AP Images, 16; Bill Waugh/AP Images, 21, 35, 38; Curtis Compton/AP Images, 23, 25, 43

Editor: Chrös McDougall
Series Designer: Craig Hinton

Library of Congress Control Number: 2014944198

Cataloging-in-Publication Data
Williams, Doug.
Tiger Woods makes Masters history / Doug Williams.
    p. cm. -- (Greatest events in sports history)
ISBN 978-1-62403-598-2 (lib. bdg.)
Includes bibliographical references and index.
1. Golf--United States--History--Juvenile literature.   2. Golfers--United States--Juvenile literature. 3. Masters Golf Tournament--Juvenile literature.   I. Title.
796.352--dc23

                                                                        2014944198

CONTENTS

CHAPTER 1

Breaking Barriers

Long before Tiger Woods made history there, Bobby Jones walked the ground in Augusta, Georgia, and had a vision. He looked out over the old nursery site and saw what would become the most beautiful golf course in the world. "It seemed that this land had been lying here for years just waiting for someone to lay a golf course upon it," he later wrote.

Jones was the greatest golfer of his era. He had been looking for a course to host a tournament for the world's best players. Jones and his partner, Clifford Roberts, bought the land in Augusta in 1931. Three years later, the first Masters Tournament was held at the Augusta National Golf Club.

Black caddies look at white golfer Gene Sarazen's golf club at the 1935 Masters.

Augusta National and the Masters would soon become legendary in the golf community. The course was known for its high quality. The greens were always fast, and the course was always beautiful and challenging. Meanwhile, the Masters became a spring tradition. Each year, golf's first major championship helped welcome the season. The world's greatest golfers arrived for the tournament each April. Some of the sport's most famous moments occurred there. But the course and the tournament also had a darker history.

Georgia and other parts of the United States were racially segregated when Augusta National opened. Blacks were barred from many facilities. For decades, Augusta National had no black members. The Masters never invited a black player, either.

Public support for segregation began to change during the 1940s. One major milestone occurred in 1947, when Jackie Robinson debuted for the Brooklyn Dodgers. He became the first black player since the 1800s to play in Major League Baseball. Yet the Professional Golfers' Association (PGA) Tour didn't drop its

THE REAL PIONEER

Lee Elder became the first black golfer to play at the Masters in 1975. However, Elder credited Charlie Sifford as the true pioneer. "Without Charlie Sifford, there would have been no one to fight the system for the blacks that followed," Elder said. He added, "Charlie was tough and hard."

"Caucasian-only" rule until 1961. The Masters, meanwhile, still did not change. As an invitational event, the Masters could set its own rules. Roberts, the longtime Masters chairman, was determined to keep blacks out. "As long as I'm alive, golfers will be white and caddies will be black," he said.

That policy kept out Charlie Sifford. Sifford was 39 in 1961 when the PGA Tour dropped its whites-only rule. He became the first black player to qualify to be a regular on the PGA Tour. He even won two tournaments in the 1960s. Yet Sifford never was invited to the Masters.

Public pressure weighed on the Masters, though. The tournament finally changed its qualification standards in 1972. Every PGA Tour winner would qualify. Two years later, black golfer Lee Elder won a PGA Tour event. That earned him a spot in the 1975 Masters.

"Some people told me, 'Man, how can you play in the Masters after all this? Why don't you refuse?'" Elder said. "But I feel I can do

Lee Elder tees off at the 1975 Masters.

more good being there. As hard as I've tried to get there, how can I run away now?"

Elder played, but not well. Yet he knew his score wasn't important. "I walked the fairways of the famous Augusta National, where they said no black man would ever play," Elder said. "In that sense, I felt I had accomplished something very important."

Later that year, across the country in California, a boy was born. As he grew, he would walk the path blazed by Sifford and Elder. And in 1997, he was among the golfers who qualified for the Masters. At birth he was named Eldrick Woods. Everybody would call him Tiger.

Tiger Woods was one of golf's rising stars when he arrived at the 1997 Masters.

CHAPTER 2

The Big
Stage

As Tiger Woods stepped out of the clubhouse at Augusta National on Tuesday of Masters week, fans flocked to him. It was April 8, 1997. The first round of the 61st Masters was still two days away. Yet fans gathered five deep around the practice green just to watch Woods putt. A huge gallery also followed his practice round.

Some simply wanted to see the sport's emerging star. At age 21, Woods hit booming drives and had a great short game. Plus, he had a big smile. He was billed as golf's next big thing. Others were drawn to him because of his potential for making history. Many believed Woods could become the first black golfer to win a tournament that had for decades been for whites only.

"Tiger Woods is to golf what Jackie Robinson was to baseball," said one fan from Atlanta who was attending his first Masters. "He is a role model for everyone. . . . The majority of people here are not African Americans, and they're following him."

Woods had turned professional the year before. Since then he had won three PGA Tour events and was named Rookie of the Year for 1996. Attendance and TV ratings improved in every tournament in which he played. Now some picked him to win the Masters over proven stars such as 1996 champion Nick Faldo and other golfing greats such as Greg Norman, Colin Montgomerie, and Tom Kite.

Yet Woods was not just any young player. He had been in the public eye since he was a toddler. He was born in

Woods, 16, follows through on a shot at the 1992 Los Angeles Open.

he turned pro. That had been his dream. As a boy, he had a poster of golfer Jack Nicklaus in his bedroom. He hoped to someday break Nicklaus's record of 18 major-tournament championships. Now in 1997 in Augusta, Woods had a chance to win his first.

Certainly, the significance of Woods winning at Augusta would be enormous. A black golfer wasn't allowed in the Masters until 1975. The club did not have its first black member until 1990. When Woods turned pro in 1996, he signed a contract with Nike to sponsor its products. In turn, Nike produced a TV commercial that introduced its client to the world. In that commercial, a portion of the script said: "Hello world. There are still courses in the US I am not allowed to play because of the color of my skin. Hello world. I've heard I'm not ready for you. Are you ready for me?"

The world was about to find out.

Woods celebrates after winning the Asian Honda Classic in February 1997. He won by a dominating 10 strokes.

Woods hits his tee shot on the second hole during the first round of the 1997 Masters.

CHAPTER 3

A Rough Start

Tiger Woods walked to the first tee for Round 1 of the Masters on April 10, 1997. He was confident. He'd just had a good week of practice. He told friends his swing and putting stroke were "clicked in."

Woods teed up his ball and took his practice swings. He then stepped up to the ball and drove it high and far. But the ball hooked far to the left of the fairway. It dropped into some trees. From there, Woods knocked the ball back into the fairway. With his third shot, he hit the green of the 410-yard par-4. He then took two putts to get the ball in the hole. That gave him a bogey. It was a bad start.

As Woods struggled in Round 1, his big gallery shrunk. A local newspaper reporter wrote about his round.

The people who gave up on Tiger Woods were wrong. Way wrong. They didn't want to watch what was happening to the magnetic young star. They didn't want to see those booming drives end up in the woods, scattering folks and leaves and pollen. They didn't want to keep glancing at the scoreboards and see his score balloon. . . . They gave up, but Woods didn't.

Source: Andy Johnston. "Tiger Strikes." Augusta Chronicle. *Chronicle Media,* April 10, 1997. Web. Accessed June 10, 2014.

Woods made pars on the next two holes. But he scored another bogey on No. 4, a par-3. He went on to finish his first nine holes with bogeys on the 8th and 9th holes. Time after time, his drives hooked left into trouble. After having such high hopes, Woods shot a 4-over-par 40 over nine holes. No Masters winner had ever had such a poor front nine.

"I was absolutely horrible out there early on," Woods said. "I was pretty ticked off after the front nine. I couldn't do anything out there. The fairways are pretty big here, but I sure couldn't hit them. I was all over the place."

Woods walks the 16th fairway during the second round of the 1997 Masters.

As Woods walked to the tee box of the 10th hole, he realized what he was doing wrong. He was taking the club too far on his backswing. That longer swing was causing him to hook the ball. He would shorten his swing.

The fix worked. The 10th hole was a par-4. Woods hit a long, straight drive. Then he hit an iron to within 18 feet of the cup. Next he made his putt. It was his first birdie of the day.

Woods made par on hole 11. Then he made birdies on holes 12 and 13. Hole 15 was a long par-5. Woods hit an enormous drive into the center of the fairway. He hit his second shot to within

YOUNG AT HEART

Woods was a professional in 1997. And he was all business on the golf course. But in many ways he was still a college kid. His family rented a house for the week of the Masters. When not golfing, Woods spent much of his time playing video games with his friends and eating burgers and fries.

four feet of the cup. Then he sank the putt for an eagle. He later added a birdie on hole No. 17.

Woods shot a 30 for his final nine holes. That meant he finished Round 1 with a 70. He was 2-under par and only three shots behind the leader. After fixing his swing, he was brilliant.

"I just tried to carry that swing feeling all the way through the back nine," Woods said.

The next day, Woods remained locked in. He birdied three holes on his front nine. Then he added two birdies and an eagle on the back nine. For the round he shot a 6-under-par 66. It was the lowest score of the first two rounds. He now had a three-shot lead over Colin Montgomerie of Scotland.

Woods's monster drives gave him an advantage on the longest holes, the par-5s. The long drives put Woods closer to the greens than most competitors. That meant he could more easily reach the greens with his second shots. Woods could use short irons that

Woods stretches in preparation to putt on the 18th green during the second round of the 1997 Masters.

gave him greater accuracy. Others were forced to use less-accurate long irons. The result: Woods was 5-under par on the course's four par-5s through two rounds.

With two rounds to go, everyone would have to catch Woods. The 33-year-old Montgomerie was hopeful that Woods's lack of experience would lead to mistakes.

"The pressure is mounting," said Montgomerie, the third-ranked golfer in the world. "I have more experience in major golf than he has. Hopefully, I can prove that."

A huge gallery watches as Woods tees off to start the third round of the 1997 Masters.

CHAPTER 4

"There Is No Chance"

Tiger Woods woke up Saturday with a three-stroke lead in the Masters. He was feeling confident after his great second round. Two more rounds remained. Woods just needed to hold on for 36 more holes and he'd be the youngest Masters champion ever at age 21. Spain's Seve Ballesteros held the record. Seventeen years earlier, he won at age 23.

Everything had changed for Woods since fixing his swing in the first round. After that, he played 27 holes in 12-under par. Stars such as Nick Faldo, Phil Mickelson, and Greg Norman had failed to qualify for the final rounds. But Woods was right where he needed to be.

After three rounds of the 1997 Masters, many sensed they were watching an event that would long be remembered. A Florida newspaper reporter captured that feeling.

Woods is on the verge of making history, and he seems determined to smash records on the way. He's on the verge of becoming the first black man to win the Masters, and the youngest man, too. . . . And this is just Woods's first major as a professional. . . . Woods isn't just routing the field, he's running up the score.

Source: Randall Mell. "It's A Runaway Tiger." SunSentinel. SunSentinel, April 13, 1997. Web. Accessed June 10, 2014.

"It's what I came here to do, to try to win the tournament," he said Friday night. But he cautioned the tournament was only half over. "I need to go out there and put up a good number tomorrow."

That's exactly what he did. He started the day at 8-under par. Then he made four birdies in his first nine holes to get to 12-under. Over the back nine, he had six pars and three more birdies. He finished his round with a birdie on the difficult 18th hole. Woods made a brilliant chip shot to put the ball within a foot of the cup before putting it in.

He shot a 7-under-par 65 for Round 3. His lead grew to nine strokes. It was the largest Masters lead after three rounds. Woods

Woods removes his tiger cover from one of his woods during the third round of the 1997 Masters.

was now 15-under par and in position to break the Masters scoring record of 17-under.

Woods said he went into Round 3 expecting someone to get hot and challenge for the lead. "I told my pop that somebody was going to make a run, shoot a 66 at the worst," he said. Woods was right. Somebody did shoot a great score. He did.

Meanwhile, the rest of the field struggled. Colin Montgomerie started the day in second place. But he shot 2-over par. Former

FATHERLY GUIDANCE

On Saturday night, Earl Woods gave his son some advice. He knew it would be hard for Tiger to concentrate on Round 4 with such a big lead. Said Earl: "Son, this will probably be one of your toughest rounds of golf you've ever had to play in your life. Just go out there and be yourself and it will be one of the most rewarding rounds you've ever played."

champions José María Olazábal and Fred Couples were both close after Round 2. But both had bad days. All over the course, players could see what Woods was doing and felt pressured to keep up.

"Everybody was trying to birdie every hole to try to catch up to him," said Davis Love III, the world's fourteenth-ranked golfer. "That's a difficult way to play."

Woods was hitting the ball farther than anyone else. He wasn't missing putts. He didn't make a single bogey.

After Round 2, Montgomerie said his experience might give him an edge. But after Round 3, he had a different opinion. "There is no chance," Montgomerie said, when asked if someone could catch Woods. "We're all human beings here. There's no chance humanly possible."

Woods makes his way to the 18th green in the third round of the 1997 Masters. The leaderboard in the background shows his runaway lead.

CHAPTER 5

Champion

Lee Elder was speeding along the highway at 85 miles per hour (137 km/h) when he saw the flashing lights of the police car behind him. After Elder pulled over, the officer had a question. Why was he going so fast? "I've got to get to the Masters," Elder said. "I have to see Tiger Woods."

Elder was the first black man to play the Masters. Until the day before his speeding ticket, he had no plans to go to Augusta in 1997. But after watching Woods in Round 3, Elder was determined to see the young golfer make history. So Elder and his wife flew to Atlanta from Florida and rented a car. Then came the speeding ticket. Despite being stopped, Elder arrived at Augusta in time. He found Woods practicing and wished him well. It was something Woods thought about as he prepared to tee off.

"He wished me good luck," Woods said. "That meant a lot to me. If it wasn't for him, I don't know if I'd ever been able to play here, or play golf, period. That did it all for me. Right then, I knew what I had to do today. I went out there with a purpose."

When Woods arrived on the first tee, the gallery was enormous. Hundreds of fans stood, one behind the other, to catch a glimpse of him. The big crowd would follow him all day, offering encouragement. Basketball star Michael Jordan was there. So was actor Jack Nicholson. Some fans were selling their tickets outside the course for as much as $10,000.

Woods made a par on his first hole. Then he had two birdies and two bogeys for an even-par 36 on the front nine. With nine more holes to go, he was 15-under par. Woods knew the tournament record, held by Jack Nicklaus and Raymond Floyd, was close. Woods wanted the record.

Woods made a 20-foot putt for a 3 on the par-4 11th hole. That put him at 16-under. On the par-5 13th hole, he hit his second shot to within 15 feet. Woods 2-putted for a birdie. That put him at 17-under. He reached the green on the par-4 14th hole in two shots.

Woods tees off on the fifth hole during the final round of the 1997 Masters.

Then Woods made an 8-foot putt for birdie to get to 18-under. The record would be his if he could at least par the final four holes.

On hole No. 15, Woods's drive drifted off the fairway. He recovered, hit the green on his third shot, and made his second putt to save a par-5. The 16th hole was a par-3. Woods barely hit the green. But he 2-putted for another par. He followed with a par on hole No. 17. Then he walked to the 18th tee knowing a victory and the record were within reach.

Woods's victory made it official: The 21-year-old was golf's new star. Media reaction around the country captured the moment.

> *This is the end of golf as we knew it. Tiger Woods obliterated it all yesterday: the hype, the records, the field in the Masters, and any doubts about his ability as the new king of the game. Woods sent the Masters' scoreboard spinning, charmed a worldwide television audience, and won one of the four biggest golf tournaments in the world by 12 strokes.*
>
> Source: C. W. Nevius. "Golf Will Never Be the Same." San Francisco Chronicle. *Hearst Communications, April 14, 1997. Web. Accessed June 10, 2014.*

Woods hit his tee shot far to the left. But his second shot hit the green. As he walked up the fairway listening to cheers, he smiled and traded high-fives with fans along the ropes.

Still, he had work to do. His first putt left him with a 4-footer for a par-4. Woods took his time. He settled over the ball. Finally, he stroked it into the hole. The moment instantly became iconic. Woods, wearing his signature red shirt and black pants, pumped his

The gallery cheers for Woods as he walks down the 6th hole during the final round of the 1997 Masters.

fist in celebration. Then, with a broad grin, he walked to the edge of the green to hug his mother and father. As Tiger and Earl Woods continued their long hug, the new Masters champion cried.

Woods had shot a final-round 3-under-par 69 to finish at a record 18-under-par 270. He was the first black Masters champion and the event's youngest and biggest winner. Since fixing his swing in Round 1, he had shot 22-under par. He beat second-place Tom Kite by a record 12 shots.

"I've never played an entire tournament with my A game," Woods said. "This was pretty close."

When Woods left the 18th green, the black champion had his arm around his white caddie. It was a scene that would have shocked former Masters chairman Clifford Roberts. Later, after watching his son slip on the green jacket of a Masters champion, Earl Woods said, "Green and black go well together, don't they?"

Tiger Woods hugs his dad, Earl Woods, after winning the 1997 Masters.

Woods poses in his green jacket while holding the
1997 Masters trophy.

CHAPTER 6

A New Era

Tiger Woods accepted his green jacket and showed off
the winner's trophy. He smiled and spoke about it being
a dream come true. But it also marked the start of a new era.
Woods had changed from promising pro to the sport's number-
one star.

TV ratings showed Woods's victory connected with viewers
across the United States. The 1997 Masters was the most-
watched golf event ever. Viewers couldn't take their eyes off
the tall, athletic golfer who hit the ball a mile and celebrated
big shots with fist pumps.

Woods continued to live up to the hype. In 2000, he won
the US Open by an amazing 15 strokes. Then he won the British
Open and the PGA Championship. He wasn't done yet, though.
The next spring, in April 2001, he won the Masters. No modern

Woods accepts the green jacket for winning the 2001 Masters. The win completed his "Tiger Slam."

golfer ever had held the titles of all four majors at once. The feat became known as the "Tiger Slam." At 25, Woods was one of the world's biggest sports stars.

"We have witnessed the greatest golfing feat of our time," Augusta National chairman Hootie Johnson said after the 2001 Masters. Woods's feat amazed even the best golfers on tour. "We're not going to ever see it again unless he does it," fellow golfer

Rocco Mediate said of the "Tiger Slam." "There's no one that's going to do that."

Through 2014, Woods had won 13 other major golf titles. Three of those were also at the Masters. Meanwhile, his 14 major victories ranked second all time to Jack Nicklaus's 18.

Woods has been equally dominant outside of the majors. He had 79 career victories on the PGA Tour through 2013. That ranked second behind only Sam Snead's 82. Woods also had been ranked number one in the World Golf Rankings more often than any other player. He also had won more money.

Woods transformed golf. His presence on tour raised TV ratings and prize money. Augusta National and other courses were made longer to "Tiger proof" them. And in the decade following the 1997 Masters, golf's image became cooler. More people took up the game, and more courses were built.

Injuries have taken a toll on Woods, however. He had knee surgery in 2008 and back surgery in 2014. He also suffered a severe slump in 2010 and 2011. He won just one event during that span after going through a divorce. Yet even at age 37 in 2013, Woods

IN THE News

was one of the best. He won five times and was selected PGA Tour Player of the Year. He also was ranked number one in the world.

Interestingly, the one aspect Woods did not change was the number of black players in pro golf. Since 1997, few black players have qualified for the PGA Tour. Meanwhile, only one black player has won an event: Woods. The doors are open now, but the sport remains expensive and not always easily accessible.

Still, Woods's 1997 victory was symbolic. A black player who once would have been barred from Augusta won the green jacket.

Woods celebrates after sinking his final putt to win the 1997 Masters.

After watching Woods win, Charlie Sifford said Woods had changed golf forever. "It's all over with now," he said. "Lee Elder played and now Tiger has won it. I'm proud of them both."

TIMELINE

March 22-25, 1934
Horton Smith wins the first Masters three years after Augusta National opens.

1961
The PGA of America removes its "Caucasian-only" clause that prohibited black players from being regular members of the PGA Tour.

1961
Charlie Sifford is the first black member of the PGA Tour.

August 20, 1967
Sifford becomes first black player to win a PGA Tour event, the Greater Hartford Open.

April 10, 1975
Lee Elder becomes first black golfer to play the Masters.

December 30, 1975
Eldrick "Tiger" Woods is born in Cypress, California.

1996
Woods wins his third consecutive US Amateur championship and a college golf national championship for Stanford.

August 1996
Woods announces he's leaving Stanford and turning professional.

April 13, 1997
Woods wins the 61st Masters.

2000-2001
Woods becomes the first golfer to win, in order, the US Open, British Open, PGA Championship, and Masters.

June 16, 2008
Woods wins his 14th major championship, the US Open, in a playoff with Rocco Mediate at Torrey Pines in San Diego, California.

2014
The total purse at the Masters is $9 million. In 1996, it was just $2.5 million.

amateur

An athlete who cannot be paid.

birdie

In golf, a score that is 1-under par, such as a 3 on a par-4 hole.

bogey

In golf, a score that is 1-over par, such as a 5 on a par-4 hole.

caddie

A person who carries a golfer's clubs, balls, tees, and other items around a course. A caddie also will offer advice about certain holes and shots.

eagle

In golf, a score that is 2-under par, such as a 3 on a par-5 hole.

endorsements

Agreements in which companies pay famous people to promote the company, its products, or both.

fairway

The area between the tee and the green where the grass is cut short on a given hole.

gallery

The crowd that follows a golfer on a course.

majors

Four yearly tournaments are designated as major tournaments for professional golfers. In chronological order, these are the Masters, the US Open, the British Open, and the PGA Championship.

par

The number of strokes assigned to a hole on a golf course. Holes are designated as par-3s, par-4s, or par-5s, meaning a good player should be able to achieve that score on that hole.

rookie

A first-year player in a league or tour.

rounds

A professional golf tournament generally consists of four rounds. Each round requires players to play all 18 holes of a course.

segregation

A social system that does not permit people of certain races to use the same facilities or have the same opportunities as others. For many decades in the Deep South of the United States, blacks could not use the same facilities as whites.

FOR MORE INFORMATION

SELECTED BIBLIOGRAPHY

Anderson, Dave. "'I'm Tight Because I Care.'" *New York Times*. The New York Times Co., April 11, 1997. Web. Accessed June 10, 2014.

Johnston, Andy. *"Elder Sees History Made."* *Augusta Chronicle*. Chronicle Media, April 14, 1997. Web. Accessed June 10, 2014.

Reilly, Rick. *"Strokes of Genius."* *SI Vault*. Time Inc., April 21, 1997. Web. Accessed June 10, 2014.

Sherman, Ed. *"Tiger Has Masters By The Tail."* *Chicago Tribune*. Tribune Co., April 12, 1997. Web. Accessed June 10, 2014.

Westin, David. *"Tiger Tracks into History."* *Augusta Chronicle*. Chronicle Media, April 13, 1997. Web. Accessed June 10, 2014.

FURTHER READINGS

Barrett, David. *Making the Masters*. New York: Skyhorse Publishing, 2012. Print.

Callahan, Tom. *His Father's Son. Earl and Tiger Woods*. New York: Gotham Books, 2010. Print.

Feinstein, John, and Rocco Mediate. *Are You Kidding me? The Story of Rocco Mediate's Extraordinary Battle with Tiger Woods at the US Open*. New York: Little, Brown and Co., Hachette Book Group, 2009. Print.

Hawkins, Jim, with Robert Hartman. *Tales from Augusta's Fairways: A Collection of the Greatest Masters Stories Ever Told*. New York: Skyhorse Publishing, 2012. Print.

WEBSITES

To learn more about the Greatest Events in Sports History, visit **booklinks.abdopublishing.com**. These links are routinely monitored and updated to provide the most current information available.

PLACES TO VISIT

United States Golf Association Museum

77 Liberty Corner Road
Far Hills, NJ 07931
(908) 234-2300
www.usgamuseum.com
Opened in 1951 in New York City, this museum was moved to New Jersey in 1972. It houses a large collection of memorabilia from top American golfers and national championships governed by the US Golf Association.

World Golf Hall of Fame

One World Golf Place
St. Augustine, FL 32092
(904) 940-4000
www.worldgolfhalloffame.org
This museum honors the contributions and accomplishments of male and female golfers from across the globe. It originally was opened in Pinehurst, North Carolina, in 1974. It moved to Florida in 1998.

INDEX

ABOUT THE AUTHOR

Doug Williams is a freelance writer and former newspaper editor. This is his fifth book. He lives in San Diego, California, with his wife and enjoys hiking, traveling, reading, and spending time with his family. As deputy sports editor of the *San Diego Union-Tribune* in 2008, he directed coverage of the 2008 US Open won by Tiger Woods.